THESE ARE OUR BODIES

FOR INTERMEDIATE

Church Publishing
NEW YORK

PARENT BOOK

Scripture from the *New Revised Standard Version Bible (NRSV)* © 1989 by the Division of Christian Education of the National Council of Churches of Christ in the USA. Used by permission.

Scripture quotations from the CEB used with permission. All rights reserved. Common English Bible, Copyright 2011.

A catalog record of this book is available from the Library of Congress.

Church Publishing Incorporated
19 East 34th Street
New York, NY 10016

Cover design by: Jennifer Kopec, 2 Pug Design
Typeset by: Progressive Publishing Services

ISBN-13: 978-0-89869-024-8 (pbk.)
ISBN-13: 978-0-89869-018-7 (ebook)

Printed in the United States of America

CONTENTS

INTRODUCTION

Welcome to *These Are Our Bodies*!

> O God, who wonderfully created, and yet more wonderfully restored, the dignity of human nature: Grant that we may share the divine life of him who humbled himself to share our humanity, your Son Jesus Christ; who lives and reigns with you, in the unity of the Holy Spirit, one God, for ever and ever. *Amen*.[1]

As Christians seeking to live a life worthy of our calling, we are called to explore our sexuality in the context of our faith. One of the greatest joys and responsibilities as parents is to teach children that they are loved by God—body and all. You and your tween have begun the *These Are Our Bodies* program.

This *Parent Book* is your first step on the journey. We know that most effective teaching about sexuality includes both children and parents. You know that your children have been watching you and learning from you since birth. Your most basic gestures, attitudes, and comments teach your children how to think about their bodies. Now that your child is close to entering (or already in) middle school, the information that they need to be informed and empowered is changing. One goal of this program is to help you communicate knowledge, skills, and values to your child and to make that vital connection between faith and sexuality.

Parents sometimes feel anxious about tackling the next stage of questions, and we want to give parents the information you need to jump right into conversations with your growing child. Although you are not the only source of information for your child, you are the primary educator—you are the most consistent, influential person in your tween's life.

We recognize that all families look different; we use "parent" in the broadest sense throughout this program. Parent refers to all those primary caretakers who have children or youth in their custody—single parents, single moms, single dads, grandparents, aunts, uncles, foster parents, adoptive parents, divorced or widowed parents, and anyone else who has responsibility for raising children. You are the one who can give them a foundation of values, attitudes, and skills that will guide them into their teenage years.

Participating in *These Are Our Bodies* paves the way for more open communication between tweens and parents, including the connection between sexuality and faith. It is a developmentally appropriate, creatively interactive, faith-based approach to sexuality that places human sexuality in the context of faith. Concepts such as God's creation, Scripture, and sexuality as a gift from God are woven throughout the sessions. The conversations and teaching around the stewardship of gifts, responsible behavior, and God's grace and love form the foundation of the theology of the program. The sessions in *These Are Our Bodies* are each designed to teach concepts around our faith in ways that connect with young people and give them opportunities to strengthen their faith.

The program includes content that makes a connection between our faith and sexuality. Participants will gain assurance that their growing and developing is normal and expected. As they continue their journey toward adulthood and independence, the program will provide opportunities to bridge the gap between their everyday lives and their lives in faith by creating a holy space for them to ask their questions and receive honest answers. The *These Are Our Bodies: Foundation Book* is the companion volume to the *These Are Our Bodies* program, including this age level called Intermediate for tweens and their caregivers. Parents are encouraged to get and read this book as well.

Your child has a *Participant Book*, which will be theirs to use during the program and to keep as a reference after the program is over. This *Parent Book* is meant to be a resource just for you. It will keep you informed about each session, informing you about what your tween is learning. You will be invited to reflect on some of the Scripture that they are studying. Each chapter also includes journal questions that will help you connect faith with sexuality and parenting. You'll learn new ways to think about sexuality and how faith is relevant to understanding the complexities of sexuality. In this program, both participants and parents learn and grow together.

Our hope is that you will talk about learning in conjunction with your tween. This program and this book work in harmony to open the lines of communication between you and your child. As we walk in faith, we benefit the most from a shared journey.

Jenny Beaumont and Abbi Long

WE ARE WONDERFULLY MADE

For it was you who formed my inward parts;
you knit me together in my mother's womb. I praise
you, for I am fearfully and wonderfully made.
Wonderful are your works; that I know very well.
—Psalm 139:13–14

In this session, your tween connected with the Psalmist's claim "I am wonderfully made," and explored the concept of being knit together in light of God's love for each of us.

The session laid the theological foundation for future sessions that focus on practical concepts such as body vocabulary and reproduction. Faith connections are what make these sessions a rich and meaningful experience for participants. Long after they have memorized the names of their body parts, they will need to know that God loves them, made them just as they are, and is always with them.

How does being made "wonderfully" make you feel?

As a parent, how does this passage resonate with you?

How does it change the way you see your tween?

We closed our first session with this litany, inspired by Psalm 139.

> God, you know me better than anyone, even myself. You know what I'm doing, you even know what I'm thinking.
> When I move around or when I lay down, when I walk or sit still, you always know where I am.
> There's nothing I say that you haven't already figured I'm going to say.
> *God, you know me inside and out.*
>
> You are in front of me to guide me, behind me to protect me, and I feel your hand on my shoulder, so I know I'm not alone. That's almost too good to be true.
> *God, you know me inside and out.*
>
> Is there anywhere I can go where you are *NOT*?
> Not any place that I know. Can I run fast enough to get away from your Spirit?
> *God, you know me inside and out.*
>
> You yourself created all my parts. You pieced me together in my mother's womb. You did an excellent job making me, and I thank you for that. You are amazing. That's for sure.
> *God, you know me inside and out.*

You've known me forever. Your eyes could see my arms and legs, even before they were fully formed. Day by day I grew bigger until I was finally me with all my parts, ready to be born.
God, you know me inside and out.

I'm amazed by your deep thoughts, O God; the number of them astounds me. I couldn't possibly count them all, because there are more of them than grains of sand on the shore. If I were to count them it would take forever, and by then I'd be as old as you.
God, you know me inside and out.

If I soar into the sky, you're there. If I lay down in the dirt, you are there too. If I fly like a bird to the middle of the biggest ocean, and then dive down into the waters, I wouldn't be surprised that you're there, too, to guide me.
God, you know me inside and out.

If I say, oh my God, I feel like it's the darkest night even in the middle of the day, I'm so sad . . . you tell me, it's alright. Dark or day, I am with you.
Figure out who I am, God. Then let me know.
Look into my deepest thoughts. I'm glad to have you here with me, to help me and lead me back to you.
God, you know me inside and out. Amen.[2]

....

2   Lynn Zill Briggs. "Psalm 139:1–23," in *God's Word, My Voice: A Lectionary for Children* (New York: Church Publishing, 2015), 233, 156. Used with permission.

WE ARE UNIQUE

Yet, O Lord, you are our Father;
we are the clay, and you are our potter;
we are all the work of your hand.
—Isaiah 64:8

In this session, your tween claimed their uniqueness in the eyes of God, explored the messages that the media and culture send around bodies and sexuality, and created personal affirmation statements about God's love for them and their uniqueness.

> Dear God, help me to live each day knowing that I am created by you. Your hand has made me and holds me tight. You are like a potter and I am like clay. Thank you for all you have done for me. Help me to remember that you are my potter not only in what I say, but in what I do as well. All praise be to you, O God. *Amen*.

In Isaiah, we read how God is the potter and we are the clay, the work of God's hand.

What does it mean to be the work of God's hands?

Think about the gentleness with which you parent. How does this gentleness reflect in your parenting? Write some of your thoughts and insights here.

Sometimes, we can forget that we are wonderfully made and that we are God's handiwork. In light of our being God's handiwork, what are some of the pressures about your body that you have experienced?

What are some expectations that you feel pressured by?

THINKING ABOUT YOUR TWEEN

What are some of the pressures you feel related to their body?

What are some expectations that you feel?

Your child explored the idea that God has created each person to do very special things. Your tween learned that we are created by God, in God's image, and declared "good" just the way we are; and your tween learned that sometimes when we begin to grow up, we become self-conscious about the way we look and compare ourselves to others.

If you were to whisper words of encouragement to your child, what would that encouragement be?

What message might God say about your tween, about their growing up, or about their body?

SOME EXAMPLES OF AFFIRMATIONS

The tweens claimed affirmations for themselves in this session. As parents, which of these affirmations do you claim?

I am the handiwork of God.

God knit me together.

God loves and accepts ME.

God loves me. So I can love me, TOO.

I know who I am and I am enough.

I am perfectly made

God loves ME!

My body is my vehicle in life; I choose to fill it with goodness.

God gave me life. I am grateful.

My life is unfolding beautifully.

God made me perfect!

I am enough, really enough, just the way I am.

My body is a gift from God.

It is not for me to decide whether my body is good enough or not.

My body is a divine gift, a temporary home for my soul.

My body and I are designed perfectly!

There is a reason I look exactly the way I look, even if I don't always like that.

What Other People Think About Me Is None of My Business!

Comparison is the thief of joy.
I am perfectly imperfect!
Life does not have to be perfect to be wonderful.
I am a child of GOD!
I am gifted.
I am gifted by GOD!
I am wonderfully made.
God made me, and God doesn't make junk.
My face is divinely created!
I am beautiful.
I am enough, I am so enough—it is unbelievable how enough I am.
My life is a wonderful journey, not a list of TO DOs.

Choose one or two affirmations to bless your tween.

Thank you God for all of these perfectly and uniquely created tweens! You are an awesome Creator. Thank you for making me the work of your hand. Sometimes I forget how cool it is to be your child. *Amen*.

WE ARE
A MIRACLE

. . . the Lord God formed the human
from the topsoil of the fertile land
and blew life's breath into his nostrils.
The human came to life.
—Genesis 2:7 (CEB)

Creator God, who through the Holy Spirit in the beginning breathed life into the nostrils of humanity, help us to wonder at the miracle of human reproduction, noticing your image imprinted on each person in the family of God, so that we may join together as your children in love and peace and grow your kingdom here on earth. *Amen*.

In this session, your child learned about human reproduction and considered the great miracle of creation. Thinking about your tween, write down the birth story or story of bringing your child home.

What were some of your thoughts and feelings when you learned that you were going to have or adopt your child?

Thinking about birth and creation as a miracle, what message or messages do you want to share with your child about their coming into the world and about raising a child?

Almighty God, giver of the miracle of life, help us leave this place and enter the world as people who see your grace at work in daily life, going to school, spending time with friends, and being a part of a community. Help us to also see the miracle of our lives, the way we were formed, the way we entered the world, and the way our bodies can make more life. For all of these things we give you thanks, through our Savior, Jesus Christ. *Amen*.

SESSION 4

WE ARE
CHANGING

Six days later, Jesus took with him Peter and James and his brother John and led them up a high mountain, by themselves. And he was transfigured before them, and his face shone like the sun, and his clothes became dazzling white. Suddenly there appeared to them Moses and Elijah, talking with him. Then Peter said to Jesus, "Lord, it is good for us to be here; if you wish, I will make three dwellings here, one for you, one for Moses, and one for Elijah." While he was still speaking, suddenly a bright cloud overshadowed them, and from the cloud a voice said, "This is my Son, the Beloved; with him I am well pleased; listen to him!" When the disciples heard this, they fell to the ground and were overcome by fear. But Jesus came and touched them, saying, "Get up and do not be afraid." And when they looked up, they saw no one except Jesus himself alone.

—Matthew 17:1–8

Divine Sustainer, who walks with us as we grow from infancy to adulthood, be present with us through all life's changes, those we welcome and those we do not, through the one whose life included both the manger and the cross, our Savior Jesus Christ. *Amen*.

The biblical passage we discussed in this session is known as the Transfiguration. Jesus and his disciples ascend a mountain to pray. What is amazing is that there on the mountaintop, the appearance of Jesus' face changes, as do his clothes. The passage concludes with a quick transition back to how Jesus appeared physically before. No more dazzling white clothes or shining face!

The passage contains a familiar statement to the reader when the voice from the cloud declares, "This is my Son, the Beloved; with him I am well pleased; listen to him!" Earlier in Jesus' life, at his baptism, a voice declares much the same.[3]

Change is a consistent part of life. Change is hard. Change takes time. Note your thoughts about the Transfiguration and change here:

....

3   Matthew 3:13, Mark 1:11, and Luke 3:22.

CHANGING PHYSICALLY, MENTALLY, AND RELATIONALLY

Your children are growing and changing. In this session, they spent time thinking about how they have changed physically, mentally, and relationally. We talked about how we change in these areas as we grow up. Think about your tween and how they have changed. Consider how you feel about those changes. Complete this chart recalling five to ten changes you have seen in your tween.

CHANGES IN THEM		
BODY	MIND	RELATIONSHIPS

Thinking about the changes that your child has undergone, why were some of your feelings negative or neutral? How might you begin to accept your child, just the way they are right now?

Journal about your how you are feeling about your child's growth.

SESSION 5

WE ARE KNOWLEDGEABLE

When Abram was ninety-nine years old, the Lord appeared to Abram, and said to him, "I am God Almighty; walk before me, and be blameless. And I will make my covenant between me and you, and will make you exceedingly numerous." Then Abram fell on his face; and God said to him, "As for me, this is my covenant with you: You shall be the ancestor of a multitude of nations. No longer shall your name be Abram, but your name shall be Abraham; for I have made you the ancestor of a multitude of nations. I will make you exceedingly fruitful; and I will make nations of you, and kings shall come from you. I will establish my covenant between me and you, and your offspring after you throughout their generations, for an everlasting covenant, to be God to you and to your offspring after you.

—Genesis 17:1–7

Holy God, you know how much we need your love. Sometimes we forget that it is always there waiting for us to accept it. Help us to remember that nothing can separate us from your love. As we spend time learning and becoming more knowledgeable, remind us of your unconditional love for us. *Amen*.

We begin each of our sessions opening with prayer and reviewing our group norms. We call this our HOLY Covenant. It is a way we honor one another in our conversations and remember that a covenant is a promise; similar to the covenants God has made with God's people, such as Abraham and Sarah.

H stands for Honesty.
O stands for Openness.
L stands for Learning Together.
Y stands for Your Questions.

Today we explored topics around human sexuality including STIs, HIV/AIDS, dating and falling in love, technology safety, sexuality, and sexual abuse—all important topics that are connected to healthy relationships. We read Genesis 17:1–7, 15–22. This is part of the biblical story of Abraham and Sarah, including their relationship to one another as well as with God. Invite your child to share what they learned about this biblical relationship.

What topics do you what to talk to your tween about? What do you want to say? Journal your thoughts here:

We played a game similar to Family Feud in which the tweens shared what they had learned about sexual health, dating, falling in love, and safety—keeping their body safe physically as well as in using technology such as the internet and cell phones.

Here is the information that we discussed that is also in their *Participant Book:*

HIV/AIDS

AIDS stands for Acquired Immunodeficiency Syndrome. It is the late stage of an infection caused by a virus that can be transmitted from an infected person to an uninfected person by an exchange of bodily fluids. HIV stands for human immunodeficiency virus. HIV is a type of STI—sexually transmitted infection. It is the virus that can lead to AIDS, if left untreated. You may hear the disease called HIV/ AIDS. HIV attacks the immune system of the body—the system that fights off disease. The virus prevents the immune system from doing its job properly, so the body is unable to defend against diseases that it may usually fight—pneumonia, for example— and some rare diseases that people with healthy immune systems seldom have because their healthy immune systems prevent illness.

Many teenagers believe that they don't have to be worried about HIV because they aren't gay or they don't use drugs. However, we should remember that if a person has sex, he or she may be exposed to the infection from their sexual partner. People can be infected with HIV if they participate in behaviors that place them at risk. These behaviors include the following:

1. Having sexual contact with an infected person
2. The sharing of needles and syringes by users of drugs

3. Unsafe ear piercing and tattooing
4. Being infected (as a mother) and passing the infection to her baby before or during birth
5. Having an unsafe blood transfusions. (People have received transfusions of blood from donors who were infected with the HIV and have become infected. However, the procedures that are now used to test blood donations have made blood transfusions in the United States very safe.)

HIV may be found in blood, semen, and vaginal fluids. The virus may enter the body of anyone coming into contact with infected fluids through sexual contact, sharing of needles, and unsafe piercing and tattooing. HIV/AIDS is not spread through casual contact. Casual contact with a person who has AIDS is not a threat to you. Using a public toilet, drinking from a fountain, and playing sports with or eating with an infected person doesn't endanger you.

Because the symptoms of HIV may not appear until long after a person has been infected, it is not always possible to tell whether or not a person has HIV. Therefore, the only way to be completely safe is to avoid behaviors that may put you at risk for HIV.

STIs

Sexually transmitted infections (STIs) are passed from one person to another through sexual contact. There are more than twenty different STIs. Some of the diseases you might hear about are syphilis, gonorrhea, chlamydia, and genital herpes. Some STIs can be treated and cured. Others are not curable, meaning that people will have the disease for life and continue to be able to pass it along to others.

The symptoms commonly associated with STIs include the following:

- Unusual discharge (leaking of thick fluid) from the penis or vagina
- Irritation, lumps, or sores on or around the genitals
- Pain or tenderness in the genitals, genital area, or abdomen
- Painful urination or frequent need to urinate

These symptoms do not automatically mean that a person has a STI. In fact, a person can have an STI and have no symptoms at all. These symptoms can also indicate the presence of other diseases—diseases that are not sexually transmitted. However, people who are sexually active and have any of these symptoms are advised to see their doctor.

WE ARE KNOWLEDGEABLE • 37

You can get an STI from sexual contact. In order to pass an STI from one body to another, there must be direct contact with the viruses or bacteria that cause the STI. This kind of contact generally happens during sexual activity. The viruses and bacteria that cause STIs are often found in bodily fluids. They are also found in places in the body that are warm and moist, such as those found in places like the penis, vulva, vagina, rectum, mouth, or throat. By touching those places on another person who has an STI, one may be infected. It is unusual for STIs to spread in ways other than human-to-human contact, like on a toilet seat. Responsible sexual behavior is the best prevention for STIs. For young people, responsible sexual behavior means waiting until they are much older to become sexually active.

Dating and Falling in Love

Dating is one way young people get to know each other. Dating is in many ways like other acts of friendship. You talk, laugh, and do things together. Friendships generally start with things that people have in common: living near each other, enjoying the same activities, or sitting beside each other in class. Friends who are dating have things in common too; the fact that they are attracted to each other adds a special element. People are drawn together because they are alike in many ways and because they are different.

When you begin to date you should learn to understand yourself, your feelings and the way your mind and body reacts when you are close to another person. Talk together about your feelings. Your ability to communicate is a sign of your maturity and readiness for dating. Be true to yourself. Show respect for yourself and for each other. God gave us gifts to share that are meant to uplift each other. Being with someone you love should make you want to be a better person, not a different person!

We were created by God to love many people, not just one. Many of the people we meet will be possible life-long partners for us, not just one. You will be meeting lots of people in the next several years. You will be developing friendships with some of the people you meet. You may want to build deeper friendships with some of those friends and eventually work at building relationships and intimacy. Perhaps there will be one special person you will decide to marry.

What questions should I ask myself to discern if I am in love?
- With whom do I enjoy spending time more than anyone else?
- Who makes me feel good about myself?
- Who do I enjoy discovering new things about?
- Who values the things I consider to be important?
- Who wants to be close to me but doesn't insist that we do everything together?

- Can I trust this person with my personal thoughts and feelings?

Infatuation is an immature, unreasonable love that is common among young people who are still new at relationships and who are searching for their own identity. Many young people confuse feelings of love with feelings of infatuation. There is nothing wrong with infatuation—it can be very exciting. But it is important not to let feelings of infatuation trick you into behaviors or commitments that really belong in mature love relationships. When you are in love, you tend to be more loving toward others and may feel like you are becoming the best person you can become through Christ's love for you. Love inspires a person to be the best they can be!

Technology Safety

Technology has given us many new ways of communicating and staying in touch with people all over the world. With this great tool, there are things we always need to keep in mind:

- Bullying via the internet, cell phone, or Facebook is still bullying. What you type is permanent. You can't take it back.
- Bullying won't help you make or keep the kind of friends that will be good friends to you.
- Anything put on the internet is public and permanent.

- Texting, email, and networking sites are not truly private or anonymous.
- People on the internet can hide their real identity.

There are many ways to use technology responsibly:
- Use the grandmother test: Don't post anything you wouldn't want your grandmother to see.
- Nothing is private! Assume anything you send or post may be sent to other people.
- Hurtful words are wrong whether you say them or type them.
- Don't give in to the pressure to do something that makes you uncomfortable, even in cyberspace.
- No regrets. Think about the feelings of other people before you text or email something that maybe unkind. You will regret hurting others.

Pornography is often found on the internet. Pornography is any image that exploits sexuality and misuses the gift of sexuality. Any picture or image that that turns people into sex objects, promotes sexual relations between children and adults, or links sex and violence together is pornography. Anytime you see sexuality being exploited, or used as a way to make money, you are probably looking at pornography. Pornography is addictive, so it is easy to sell once a person's normal curiosity gets "hooked." If you see pictures or get onto a website that you know shows pornography, tell your parents immediately.

Sexual Abuse

Much attention has been given to the subject of sexual abuse. We are beginning to recognize that the problem is widespread. We have been telling children to be careful of strangers, but we haven't told them why. We're trying to do a better job of informing young people about the dangers of sexual abuse in hopes that greater awareness will decrease the problems.

To abuse something is to use it in an improper or destructive way. Sex abusers use sex in an improper and destructive way. Most often people who are abusive are misusing their power to hurt someone else. They also may have been abused themselves as children and be confused about the place of sex in their lives. In most cases, sex abusers are acquaintances— even friends and relatives. Most sex abusers are men, but women can be abusive as well. Because it is against the law to abuse a person sexually, sex abusers are guilty of a sexual crime.

You are in control of your body. Anytime anyone touches you or asks you to do things related to sex that make you feel uncomfortable, tell them to stop. Then, share your feelings with a trustworthy adult. Your friends should do the same thing, if they find themselves in this situation.

Talk with your child about your thoughts about such topics, and ask them to share their insights and learnings.

WE ARE COMPLEX

Love is patient; love is kind;
love is not envious or boastful or arrogant or rude.
It does not insist on its own way;
it is not irritable or resentful;
it does not rejoice in wrongdoing, but rejoices in the truth.
It bears all things, believes all things,
hopes all things, endures all things.
—1 Corinthians 13:4–7

Most Holy God, who invites us to live as people of love and grace, help us to see you at work as we seek to understand how we are each unique. *Amen*.

In this session, our tweens learned about gender stereotypes (especially those related to the human body), considered what gender norms they embrace and reject, and developed their understanding of their own gender identity and gender expression.

Gender is a word we use to talk about others and ourselves. Gender is felt inside of ourselves and expressed to others. When we show or express to others our gender, we call that gender expression. When we feel or sense our gender in our minds and hearts, we call that gender identity.

Sometimes, people think gender is the same as biological sex, or they think it refers to whether a person is male, female, or a born with both male and female organs. Gender is separate.

Journal about some thoughts that come up for you when thinking about gender.

This is a quiz that the tweens took to consider their perceptions of gender roles and conformity. The answers were also given to help the tweens think about each topic.

"I" QUIZ

1. When I get dressed in the morning, I usually think about . . .
   a. my overall look.
   b. whether I will stand out.
   c. if I have a "cool" outfit on.
   d. only what I want and just grab something.
   e. All of the above

ANSWER: No matter what you decide to wear, you are a child of God! Clothes can be an expression of how we feel about ourselves. Try to avoid falling into the trap of our culture that says how you look is who you are. You are so much more than your clothes, hair, and physical appearance. Sometimes, we use clothes to express our gender to others, and that is OK. Have you ever thought about that before? Record some of your thoughts about why you dress the way you do. Consider sharing them with your parents.

2. I like to mainly wear the color . . .
   a. red.
   b. blue.
   c. black.
   d. pink.
   e. None of the above

ANSWER: Can colors really be assigned to one group of people? Aren't colors a "neutral" category? Think about why you wear a certain color most of the time. Is it because you like that color? Is it because it is a favorite sports team's color? Do you even get to choose, or is it whatever your parents buy you? The key to expressing yourself is feeling free to be YOU, fully you! If wearing a color that many people think is only for "girls" or only for "boys" makes you feel more like yourself, consider talking to your parents about it.

3. Even though my classmates sometimes _____, I don't feel comfortable doing it.
   a. wear makeup
   b. play sports
   c. wear skirts
   d. grow their hair long
   e. _____ (Make up your own response.)

ANSWER: The choices on this list are often associated with one group of people. Ask yourself, why don't I feel comfortable wearing makeup? Why don't I feel comfortable playing sports? Why don't I feel comfortable wearing skirts? Why don't I feel comfortable grow their hair long? Does it have anything to do with how you express your gender? Write about your thoughts here.

4. When I think about how I feel, I would say . . .
   a. I feel mostly like a girl.
   b. I feel mostly like a boy.
   c. I don't know how I feel about my gender.

ANSWER: Gender identity is the way you feel about yourself. If you have questions about this, talk to your parents. Talk to a leader in your church or the facilitator of this program.

5. I feel like my body_____.

ANSWER: Your tween wrote down some things about their growing and changing body. Use this quiz as a way to open up conversation around their growing and changing body.

God, help us feel your love. When we feel lonely or afraid, help us find strength to be brave. Help us to share our fears and hopes with others. *Amen.*

WE ARE EQUIPPED

But each of us was given grace according to the measure of Christ's gift. Therefore it is said, "When he ascended on high he made captivity itself a captive; he gave gifts to his people." The gifts he gave were that some would be apostles, some prophets, some evangelists, some pastors and teachers, to equip the saints for the work of ministry, for building up the body of Christ, until all of us come to the unity of the faith and of the knowledge of the Son of God, to maturity, to the measure of the full stature of Christ. We must no longer be children, tossed to and fro and blown about by every wind of doctrine, by people's trickery, by their craftiness in deceitful scheming. But speaking the truth in love, we must grow up in every way into him who is the head, into Christ, from whom the whole body, joined and knitted together by every ligament with which it is equipped.

—Ephesians 4.7–8 and 10–16

Holy God, for the gift of our children we give you thanks. When we think of how they have grown, we stand in awe. Remind us of your constant presence in our lives. Remind us that you experienced our same joys and struggles through the miracle of your incarnation. Guide us as we journey together through this program. In Jesus' name. *Amen*.

After reading chapter 21 in *These Are Our Bodies: Foundation Book*, "Parents are the Key," journal about some of your thoughts.

What takeaways did you have from your reading and discussion?

Tweens can be filled with questions. Some tweens seem to be in constant question mode, while others have started to hesitate when they are unsure. All children benefit from the experiences and support systems that help them to navigate and thrive in the world as they grow into adults. Learning to answer questions is integral to building the connection between parent and child.

We can use the F.O.C.U.S. acronym to answer questions.

F—Find a way to get on their level.

When an adult sits next to a tween or joins them on their level, it shows that child you are attending to them and that you are present. It may not be as comfortable for you. You are also providing a kinder, gentler environment for the tween to express their wonders or their worries.

O—Be open to the conversation.

Be patient. Adjust your tone of voice. Check your own feelings, emotions, or past experiences. Remember that this is your child's journey. At this age, adults have to work hard to overcome the desire of the tween to assert independence through their thinking. Often tweens are not excited about talking to their parents. Be patience as they speak. Wait until they get to their point. Try not to interrupt them, especially if you disagree or feel alarmed.

C—Clarify with questions or statement.

Ask clarifying questions. Use statements to help your tween tell you more. For example, "Tell me more about that. That sounds tough."

U—Use accurate language to answer their questions.

Seek to use words or explanations that explain the topic in an accurate way. Holding back information only allows someone else to fill in the cracks later. That someone may be a friend, or another adult, but it might also be a kid on the back of the bus. If the topic is complex, make a mental note to come back to the discussion at a later time.

S—Share a faith connection.

The last piece adds a faith connection that links questions about our bodies and sexuality to our Christian life together. These are both implicit and explicit messages that (a) model to our children how our faith intersects with our sexuality and (b) lay a foundation for our lives as Christians. Our faith also informs and guides our choices, attitudes, and behaviors. Making these faith connections helps us to ask, "Where is God in this?"

Divide into groups of three or four, and share what jumps out to you about this model. What would be the most challenging?

HOMEWORK FOR NEXT SESSION

Take this model of answering questions away with you, and look for a teachable moment this week to practice. At our next session, we will talk about your experiences and learn from one another.

Journal about your using the F.O.C.U.S. method. How did it go?

O God, you have prepared for those who love you such good things as surpass our understanding: Pour into our hearts such love towards you, that we, loving you in all things and above all things, may obtain your promises, which exceed all that we can desire; through Jesus Christ our Lord, who lives and reigns with you and the Holy Spirit, one God, for ever and ever. *Amen.*[4]

SESSION 8

WE ARE CALLED

O Lord, you have taught us that without love whatever we do is worth nothing; Send your Holy Spirit and pour into our hearts your greatest gift, which is love, the true bond of peace and of all virtue, without which whoever lives is accounted dead before you. Grant this for the sake of your only Son Jesus Christ, who lives and reigns with you and the Holy Spirit, one God, now and for ever. *Amen*.[5]

When we parent with our faith as the foundation, we are led to look out in front of our everyday experiences to teach and led our children to the best self that they can be. In this session, we will think about how we can lay the foundation for what we would like our family and our children to be like in five, ten, or twenty years. We will examine how our conversations today can build stronger relationships with our children and give them the tools and experiences they need to grow and develop.

"After these things Jesus showed himself again to the disciples by the Sea of Tiberias; and he showed himself in this way. Gathered there together were Simon Peter, Thomas called the Twin, Nathanael of Cana in Galilee, the sons of Zebedee, and two others of his disciples. Simon Peter said to them, 'I am going fishing.' They said to him, 'We will go with you.' They went out and got into the boat, but that night they caught nothing.

Just after daybreak, Jesus stood on the beach; but the disciples did not know that it was Jesus. Jesus said to them, 'Children, you have no fish, have you?' They answered him, 'No.' He said to them, 'Cast the net to the right side of the boat, and you will find some.' So they cast it, and now they were not able to haul it in because there were so many fish. That disciple whom Jesus loved said to Peter, 'It is the Lord!' When Simon Peter heard that it was the Lord, he put on some clothes, for he was naked, and jumped into the lake. But the other disciples came in the boat, dragging the net full of fish, for they were not far from the land, only about a hundred yards off.

When they had gone ashore, they saw a charcoal fire there, with fish on it, and bread. Jesus said to them, 'Bring some of the fish that you have just caught.' So Simon Peter went aboard and hauled the net ashore, full of large fish, a hundred and fifty-three of them; and though there were so many, the net was not torn. Jesus said to them, 'Come and have breakfast.' Now none of the disciples dared to ask him, 'Who are you?' because they knew it was the Lord. Jesus came and took the bread and gave it to them, and did the same with the fish. This was now the third time that Jesus appeared to the disciples after he was raised from the dead."

—John 21:1–14

What if Jesus is asking the disciples to bring the gifts—their material gifts and their whole selves? The disciples were asked to contribute their gift and bring their entire selves to contribute to God's work. They come with mind, *body*, and soul.

It seems that Jesus has chosen us to be part of bringing the kingdom of God to the here and now. *All* of ourselves—God is calling to us and asking that we bring our mind, *body*, and soul to build up the kingdom of God.

- How does it feel to consider that we are an integral part of Jesus' kingdom building?
- Think about the children in your home. What gifts might God have given them to build the kingdom?
- What is the difference between giving a preference to nurturing a child's mind versus their body?
- What is the difference between giving a preference to nurturing a child's body versus their mind?
- How can we nurture our children's minds, souls, and *bodies*?

WHY WE DO THINGS MATTERS, TOO: GENDER STEREOTYPES

Thinking about sexuality and our sexual expression, we often hear redirection like, "that is not ladylike" or "that is not gentlemanly." Using gender divisive language sets up a double standard based on gender. Do we really have different standards based on gender?

Don't we want all people to be helpful and kind, compassionate and empathetic, and courageous? One night around the dinner table, my husband challenged our son to eat a lemon in its entirety. The evening meal was transformed into a loud contest of courage and excitement! At the end of the contest, when the lemon had been eaten skin and all, my husband declared, "You just earned a man card." Everyone was very animated. Then the youngest and only girl, at the time just seven, asked, "What's a boy card?" Then she quickly demanded, "I want a girl card."

Her question was a challenge to our understanding of tenacity and courage. How could we define what a "boy card" meant in our family and create room for a "girl card" as well? It isn't easy to rethink the ways that define manhood and womanhood and to find ways to lift up humanness in all its forms. Our wonders shifted at that dinner. What were we teaching by daring children to perform a feat? Was this a harmless bit of fun, and how could we re-craft our message? What was a man card or boy card, and what was a girl card or woman card? What did they stand for, and if these were not the values we wanted to instill? What did we want to teach about being a person in this world? How can we all be our full selves?

Naming the values that lie behind our attitudes and concerns helps us to align our actions, teaching, and behaviors with our faith.

- What do you want your children to know about being male or female?
- How could those messages be confining or limiting to your children?

In the next month, think about the values that you are modeling with your children. Look for and name the gifts that God has given the children in your care.

> Jesus said, "You are the light of the world. A city built on a hill cannot be hid. No one lights a lamp to put it under a bucket, but on a lamp-stand where it gives light for everyone in the house. And you, like the lamp, must shed light among your fellow men, so that they may see the good you do, and give glory to your Father in heaven."
>
> —Matthew 5:14–16

> Almighty and everliving God, in your tender love for the human race you sent your Son our Savior Jesus Christ to take upon him our nature, and to suffer death upon the cross, giving us the example of his great humility: Mercifully grant that we may walk in the way of his suffering, and also share in his resurrection; through Jesus Christ our Lord, who lives and reigns with you and the Holy Spirit, one God, for ever and ever. *Amen*.[6]

....

WE ARE BUILDING A CONTAINER

Blessed be the God and Father of our Lord Jesus Christ, who has blessed us in Christ with every spiritual blessing in the heavenly places, just as he chose us in Christ before the foundation of the world to be holy and blameless before him in love. He destined us for adoption as his children through Jesus Christ, according to the good pleasure of his will, to the praise of his glorious grace that he freely bestowed on us in the Beloved.

—Ephesians 1:3–6

Almighty God, you have poured upon us the new light of your incarnate Word: Grant that this light, enkindled in our hearts, may shine forth in our lives; through Jesus Christ our Lord, who lives and reigns with you, in the unity of the Holy Spirit, one God, now and for ever. *Amen.*[7]

We are going to consider how we can support our tweens in the years to come as they build a container, or identity for themselves, and how we as parents can give them the opportunity to struggle and grow. The stories of our faith bind us together over time and space.

Anne Kitch reminds us that our baptism binds us together as the Body of Christ, called to grow in [our] understanding of God's will for [us], to develop a moral stance based on the teachings of Christ, and to become a more loving people.[8]

There is space at the table and space in the river Jordan for all to participate in the conversation, even if we do not agree. We are not called to be of one mind; we are called, with God's help, to love our neighbors and to respect the dignity of every

7   Book of Common Prayer, 213

8   Anne E. Kitch. *Taking the Plunge: Baptism and Parenting* (New York: Morehouse Publishing, 2006), xiv.

human being. Honoring the body recognizes and embraces humans as sexual beings.

WHAT CONTAINER ARE WE BUILDING?

We have been in union with God and Christ from the beginning. Whole and perfect. That is sometimes hard to believe and impossible to remember. In his Letter to the Ephesians, Paul states, "Just as he chose us in Christ before the foundation of the world to be holy and blameless before him in love."[9] Our children can also struggle to accept the blessing that God has bestowed on each of us. When people do not find their unity in God, they struggle with the mere substitutes that promise substance. Our children need a safe place to recognize their connection to God—to learn that connection will sustain them body, mind, and soul.

Consider our bodies as they physically carry us through life, helping us engage and make sense of the world. We cannot separate one part of our bodies from another; therefore, we cannot separate our sexuality from our bodies. Our body, our sexuality, our whole person is called into life and ministry.

....

9   See Ephesians 1:3–6.

Stephanie Paulsell writes:

> Young people who have grown up learning that the body mirrors back to us something important about God and that the body's desires are a precious gift from God worthy of being sheltered and allowed to develop in freedom have a compass to help them negotiate the road to sexual maturity.
>
> Adolescence will never be easy. And our world holds dangers that are sometimes beyond our power to control. But young people who have learned to honor their bodies in every other aspect of their lives will be more convinced that their bodies and the bodies of others are deserving of honor in their sexual lives as well. They will be better equipped to resist that which would diminish them or constrain their freedom to become the people they were meant to be, and better able to embrace that which would enlarge their spirits and nurture an ever more loving engagement with the world.[10]

This idea that in our young years we need to search for and find our identity is evident in psychology and in theology. In *Falling Upward*, Richard Rohr writes about the two halves of life. The task of the first half is for us to build a "container" to hold the

----

10 Stephanie Paulsell. *Honoring the Body: Meditations on a Christian Practice* (San Francisco: Jossey-Bass, 2002), 154.

contents of the second half of life. We build this "container" by struggling with law, tradition, custom, authority, boundaries, and morality, as we have to have something hard and half-good to rebel against. The first half of life is hard enough.[11]

The container is filled with our occupation, opinion, positions, ego, self, and identity into our second half of life. We need a strong container—a place to learn, grow and to fight against. The struggle secures our identity and sense of self.

As part of our calling as parents and guides to young people, we have an opportunity to help those in the first half of life build a strong enough "container."

How might we as parents give our tweens the boundaries that they need and the freedom to grow and learn?

1. How might our bodies model back something about God?
2. How might we instill a sense of honoring the body in our tweens? How might this value help our tweens as they grow?
3. What adult mentors did you have as a child or teen? What insights or learnings did you glean from those relationships?
4. What "container" do you wish to build for your child?

....

11 Adapted from *These Are Our Bodies: Foundation Book*, 37.

In the next few weeks, consider, "What container do you want to build for your child?" Journal some of your ideas here:

Almighty God, by your Holy Spirit you have made us one with your saints in heaven and on earth: Grant that in our earthly pilgrimage we may always be supported by this fellowship of love and prayer, and know ourselves to be surrounded by their witness to your power and mercy. We ask this for the sake of Jesus Christ, in whom all our intercessions are acceptable through the Spirit, and who lives and reigns for ever and ever. *Amen*.[12]

....

12   Book of Common Prayer, 250

WE ARE MATURING

⁴¹Now every year his parents went to Jerusalem for the festival of the Passover. ⁴²And when he was twelve years old, they went up as usual for the festival. ⁴³When the festival was ended and they started to return, the boy Jesus stayed behind in Jerusalem, but his parents did not know it. ⁴⁴Assuming that he was in the group of travelers, they went a day's journey. Then they started to look for him among their relatives and friends. ⁴⁵When they did not find him, they returned to Jerusalem to search for him. ⁴⁶After three days they found him in the temple, sitting among the teachers, listening to them and asking them questions. ⁴⁷And all who heard him were amazed at his understanding and his answers. ⁴⁸When his parents saw him they were astonished;

and his mother said to him, "Child, why have you treated us like this? Look, your father and I have been searching for you in great anxiety." [49]He said to them, "Why were you searching for me? Did you not know that I must be in my Father's house?" [50]But they did not understand what he said to them. [51]Then he went down with them and came to Nazareth, and was obedient to them. His mother treasured all these things in her heart. [52]And Jesus increased in wisdom and in years, and in divine and human favor.

—Luke 2:41–52

DISCUSSION QUESTIONS

- What must have been difficult for Jesus' parents?
- How might Jesus have felt in the temple learning from and teaching the priests and scribes?
- How do children and tweens find themselves "increased in wisdom and in years, and in divine and human favor?" What might that mean today?
- Parents: How have you seen your tween increase in wisdom and in years, and in divine and human favor?
- Tweens: How have you increased in wisdom and in years, and in divine and human favor?
- Parents: How have you as an adult increased in wisdom and in years, and in divine and human favor?

INTERVIEW QUESTIONS FOR YOUR TWEEN

- What is your favorite thing to do?

- What do you like best about our family? Why?

- What are you looking forward to about growing up?

- How do you feel about the physical changes you're experiencing now?

- Do you feel that you can talk to me about anything?

- Do you feel we've discussed the kinds of things that concern you about going through puberty and growing up?

- What kinds of things do you think parents and their children need to talk about?

- What do you think is the greatest pressure facing young people your age today?

CLOSING

A Reading from Matthew 5:14–16:

Jesus said, "You are the light of the world. A city built on a hill cannot be hid. No one lights a lamp to put it under a bucket, but on a lamp-stand where it gives light for everyone in the house. And you, like the lamp, must shed light among your fellow men, so that they may see the good you do, and give glory to your Father in heaven."

Leader: The Lord be with you.

Participants: And also with you.

Leader: Let us pray.

Dear gracious and loving God, who knows the joy of tweens, parents, and family. Our hearts are full of gratitude for these parent and tweens here today. We thank you for the gifts that you have given them and the light that they bring into the world through your grace. Help them to fill their homes with the light of your love and keep them ever closer to each other and to you. In your Son's name we pray. *Amen*.

RESOURCES

Authors' note to parents
These Are Our Bodies: Foundation Book has an extensive glossary, bibliography, and overview of child development that we recommend for your own information as well as to support and understand your child.

Organizations
- **Advocates for Youth:** Helps young people make informed and responsible decisions about their reproductive and sexual health; offers lessons and curricula. www.advocatesforyouth.org/sex-education-home
- **The Center for Lesbian & Gay Studies in Religion and Ministry:** Has a mission to advance the well-being of lesbian, gay, bisexual, queer, and transgender people and to transform faith communities and the wider society by taking a leading role in shaping a new public discourse on religion, gender identity, and sexuality through education, research, community building, and advocacy. http://clgs.org

- **The Coalition for Positive Sexuality**: Offers information in English and Spanish for young people who are sexually active or considering sexual activity. http://positive.org
- **Common Sense Media**: A trusted media education resources offers questions and answers regarding privacy and the internet. www.commonsensemedia.org/privacy-and-internet-safety
- **Faith Trust Institute**: A national, multi-faith, multicultural training and education organization that works to end sexual and domestic violence. www.faithtrustinstitute.org
- **Integrity USA**: An organization "proclaiming God's inclusive love in and through the Episcopal Church since 1975." www.integrityusa.org
- **Religious Institute**: A multi-faith organization dedicated to advocating for sexual health, education, and justice in faith communities and societies. www.religiousinstitute.org
- **Stop Bullying**: Information, videos, lessons, and more to respond to bullying. www.stopbullying.gov
- **Trans Student Educational Resources**: A youth-led organization dedicated to transforming the educational environment for transgender and gender nonconforming students through advocacy and empowerment. In addition to creating a more transgender-friendly education system, their mission is

to educate the public and teach transgender activists how to be effective organizers. TSER believes that justice for transgender and gender nonconforming youth is contingent on an intersectional framework of activism. Ending oppression is a long-term process that can only be achieved through collaborative action. www.transstudent.org

Print resources
- Laura Berman. *Talking to Your Kids About Sex: Turning "The Talk" into a Conversation for Life*. New York: DK Publishing, 2009.
- Stephanie Brill and Rachel Pepper. *The Transgender Child: A Handbook for Families and Professionals*. San Francisco, CA: Cleis Press, 2008.
- Robert C. Dykstra, Allan Hugh Cole Jr., and Donald Capps. *Losers, Loners, and Rebels: The Spiritual Struggles of Boys*. Louisville, KY: Westminster John Knox Press, 2007.
- Robie H. Harris. *It's Not the Stork!: A Book About Girls, Boys, Babies, Bodies, Families and Friends*. Somerville, MA: Candlewick Press, 2008.
- Robie H. Harris. *It's So Amazing!: A Book About Eggs, Sperm, Birth, Babies, and Families*. Somerville, MA: Candlewick Press, 2014.